THE MONKEY CREW SERIES

Coconut Crushers: Jungle Jam Champs

Written and Illustrated by

DEBBIE BLOWER

© 2025 Debbie Blower. All rights reserved.
No part of this book may be reproduced, stored in a retrieval system, or transmitted in any form or by any means—electronic, mechanical, photocopying, recording, or otherwise—without prior written permission of the publisher, except in the case of brief quotations embodied in critical articles and reviews.

First Edition 2025

ISBN: 978-0-9739637-5-5

Printed in Canada
For information, contact:
debbieblowerpublishing@gmail.com
Debbie Blower Publishing

This is a work of fiction. The monkeys, trucks, and jungle are all products of imagination. Any resemblance to real persons or events is purely coincidental.

Dedication

For my wonderful grandsons—Wesley, Blake, Owen, and Miles—the real Monkey Crew.

May you always race forward with joy, curiosity, determination, and love.

This adventure is yours!

With all my love,
Nana

Character Map

Owen
The Determined Dynamo

Blake
The Curious Explorer

Wesley
The Gentle Leader

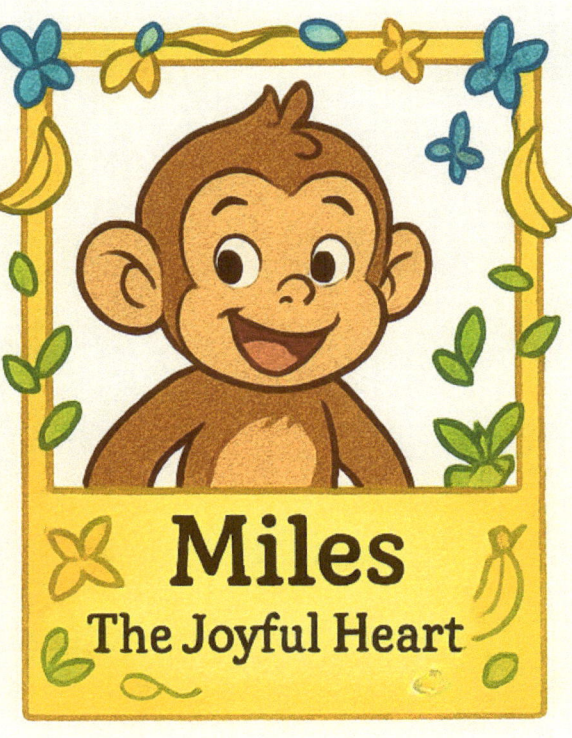

Miles
The Joyful Heart

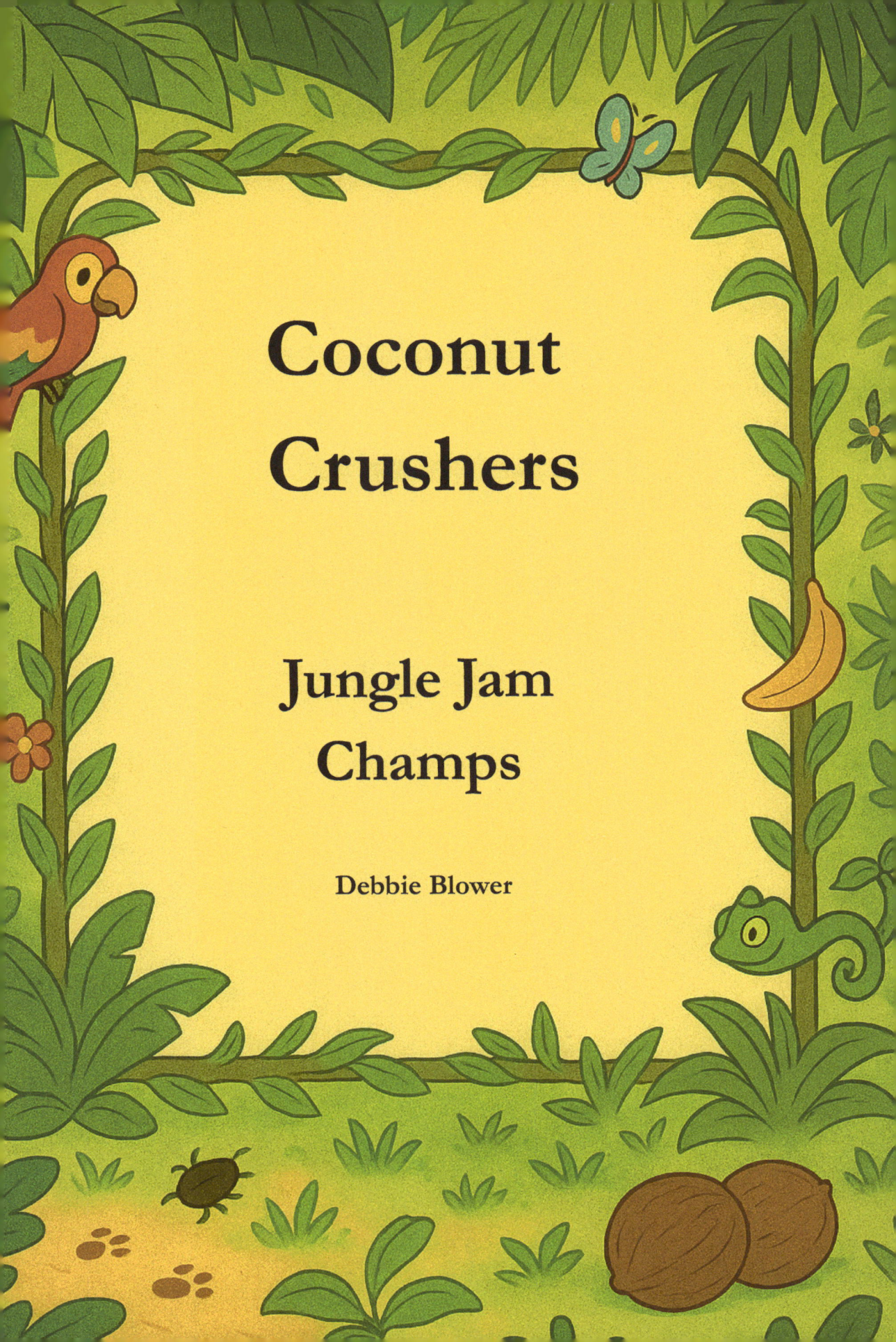

One sunny morning in the heart of the jungle, the Monkey Cousins were playing tag beneath the towering palm trees. Laughter echoed through the vines, and giggles bounced off the tree trunks. Suddenly, Blake skidded to a stop, his big eyes widening as he spotted something shiny flapping in the breeze, pinned to the side of a tall tree.

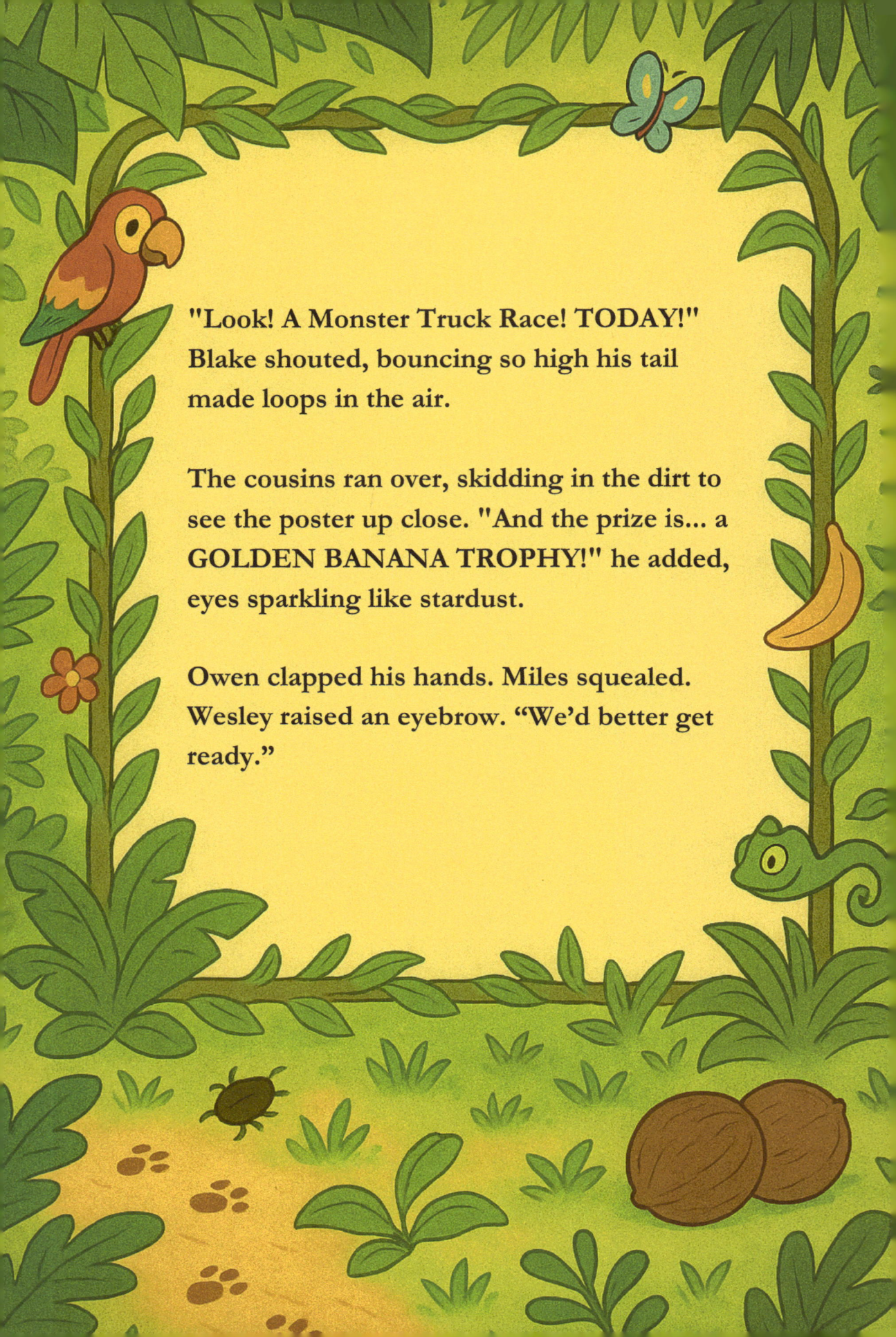

"Look! A Monster Truck Race! TODAY!" Blake shouted, bouncing so high his tail made loops in the air.

The cousins ran over, skidding in the dirt to see the poster up close. "And the prize is... a **GOLDEN BANANA TROPHY!**" he added, eyes sparkling like stardust.

Owen clapped his hands. Miles squealed. Wesley raised an eyebrow. "We'd better get ready."

Wesley rubbed his chin thoughtfully. "But we don't have monster trucks," he said. "Not yet." He looked around the jungle and smiled. "We'll have to build our own.

We've got coconuts, vines, and plenty of monkey muscle!" Owen punched the air. "Let's get to work!"

Wesley crouched down and sketched blueprints in the sandy soil. "We'll use coconut shells for the body, vines for ropes and harnesses, and wheels from our old jungle scooters," he explained.

"Don't forget decorations!" Blake added, already sticking leaves to a helmet. "Let's build the best coconut monster trucks the jungle's ever seen!"

Each monkey built a unique truck. Wesley's was strong, square, and sturdy—designed for balance and control, with thick wheels and reinforced branches for the frame.

Blake's was wild and colorful, complete with a periscope made from a bamboo tube, leaf flags, and banana peel flames painted on the sides.

Owen's truck had vine-powered boosters that shot bursts of jungle air. He zipped in wild circles, leaving muddy skid marks and startled squirrels in his wake.

Miles's was small but mighty—perfectly balanced with smooth-rolling wheels, acorn headlights, and banana mirror blinkers that twinkled in the sunlight.

"Let's race!" Owen whooped.

They rolled their trucks to the starting line, hearts pounding. Around them, racers from every part of the jungle were ready to rumble.

"3… 2… 1… GO!" squawked the toucan. Engines roared. The Monkey Cousins launched into the jungle, leaves flying, tires spinning, cheers shaking the treetops.

Owen zoomed over a hill and soared through the air—

WHAM! He landed sideways and spun into a viney tangle. "Ack!"

Blake darted into a shortcut. "Follow me!"

But vines grabbed his wheels, and his periscope clogged with leaves. "Nope! Bad idea!"

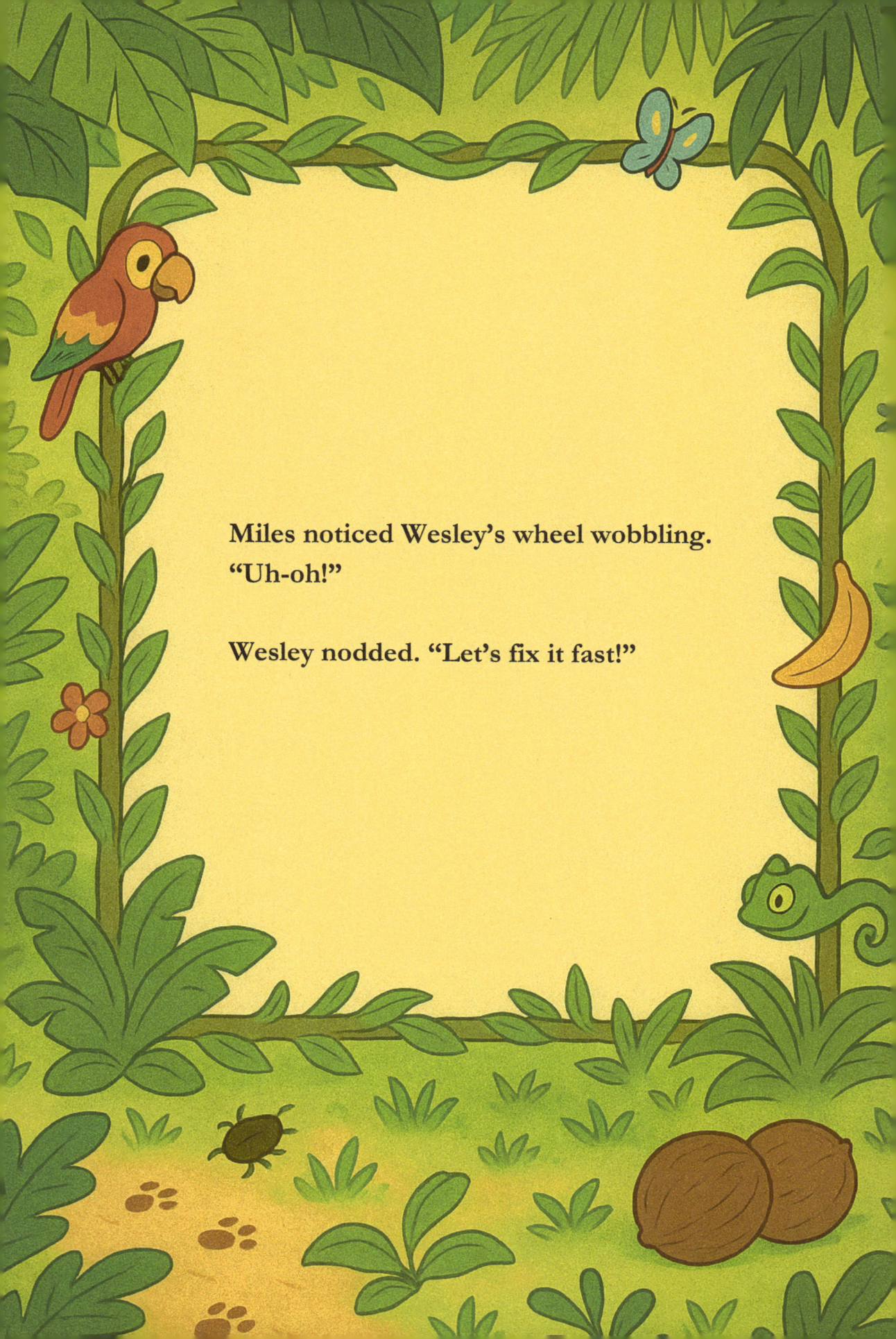

Miles noticed Wesley's wheel wobbling. "Uh-oh!"

Wesley nodded. "Let's fix it fast!"

Vines twisted. Wheel tightened.
"Let's roll!"

Wesley and Miles zipped forward,
determination in their eyes.

The cousins regrouped just past a fallen log.
Owen pulled off vines. Blake wiped off banana goo.

"Team Coconut's back!" Wesley shouted.

They jumped into position.

But as they neared the final hill, they saw how far behind they were.

"We'll never catch up," Blake muttered.

Owen slumped. "We're out of boosters."
.
Wesley glanced back. "Unless…"
He smiled. "We finish like we started—together."

Up ahead, a speedy lemur zipped into the mango mudslide, drums pounding from his truck.

"He's gonna win!" Owen gasped.

"Not if Team Coconut has anything to say!" Blake grinned.

They lined up, side by side.
"Let's go!"

The mudslide was wild—slippery, gooey, full of flying mango pits. Wesley led. Owen boosted. Blake spun. Miles bounced. Their laughter echoed louder than the chaos.

In the final stretch, the lemur's wheels hit a mango pit—SPLAT!

He flipped sideways!

The cousins shot past him, yelling, "TOGETHER!"

They crossed the finish line side by side in a flurry of petals and cheers.

"We did it!" Blake shouted.

"We did it together!" Wesley beamed.

"You didn't win by being fastest," said the toucan, placing the golden banana trophy in their hands.
"You won by being a team."

The cousins roared and raised it high.

"And for our happiest driver," the toucan grinned, "a special prize goes to… Miles!"

Miles clapped and laughed as he received a smiling mango trophy.

That night, the jungle partied with banana smoothies and mango cupcakes.

"We should totally do this again," Owen said.

"Next time," Blake added, "I'm adding rocket boosters!"

Under the starlit sky, the cousins sat on their trucks and gazed upward. Blake raised his smoothie.

"To Team Coconut—the best racers, the best builders, and the best cousins."

www.ingramcontent.com/pod-product-compliance
Lightning Source LLC
Chambersburg PA
CBHW041543040426
42446CB00003B/217